Crucibles
Refinement of the Neophyte Christian

by Branch Isole

Copyright © 2008

Crucibles
Refinement of the Neophyte Christian
by Branch Isole

Printed in the United States of America

Library of Congress Control Number:
2004114530
ISBN 0-9747692-3-1
ISBN 978-09747692-3-3

Mana'o Publishing
www.manaopublishing.com

MANA'O PUBLISHING
Lahaina, Maui, Hawaii

Order additional copies of this book at
www.fellowship-of-believers.com
or www.manaopublishing.com

"I have refined you, though not as silver;
I have tested you in the furnace of affliction."

~Isaiah 48:10

Contents

Introduction

A *Crucible* is most notably a vessel in which substances are subjected to intense temperatures in a process of refinement, thus burning away impurities while producing a newer more viable creation. It is a severe condition whereby different elements react resulting in a new born identity. This is also the case for the new believer or 'Neophyte' Christian, as different aspects of matter and spirit are combined to bring about a new creation in Christ.

Although Jesus as teacher makes his thoughts, words and deeds easier to understand through interaction between the Neophyte and Holy Spirit, once this 'choice of conversion' has been made, the fire of doubt and denial is often turned up for the new Christian.

Every Neophyte Christian faces a myriad of trials and tribulations in the form of temptations, pressures and questions after their election to become a new believer and follower of Jesus the Christ.

The Neophyte in this early stage of Christian growth as a new believer may be most susceptible to the tests of his or her life altering decision. With big eyes and bigger expectations, the Neophyte Christian can be blindsided by a world not ready to give up another soul to a relationship with God's Holy Spirit.

For the searching and struggling
individual who has come to Christianity with an
open heart and mind believing all has been
righted and there will be clear sailing ahead,
realities may produce a trauma as startling as a
wooden club to the forehead.

One of the more confusing issues
for Christians is an understanding of the
'responsibility of action' found in the teachings
of Jesus Christ. For many Christians, 'Christ-
like' behavior is neither part nor parcel of their
spiritual wisdom or daily actions. This
observation may prove to be both incompatible
and discouraging for the Neophyte Christian.

May these thoughts of refinement
produce uplifting solace and fortitude for every
Neophyte believer discouraged by the afflictions
of Christianity's trials and tests.

Branch Isole

It was as if I were a child
on the seashore picking up shells
while the great ocean of truth
lay undiscovered before me

~ Isaac Newton

Above and Below

For many it's about material goods
and efforts to acquire more 'stuff'
For far too many
no matter how much, still
it's never enough

Their possessions supply an identity
reasons, excuses
of who and how
they are perceived to be
Believing these will fill the void
that yearning deep within
Too often however
only homes and garages are filled
their content rewards excessively thin

Emptiness within the heart
can only be filled with love
The love of original spark
that for mortal man
resides above

Love, a misnomer
we use and abuse
in this time and place
To describe our lustful
temporal desires
found on the growing lists of acquisitions
for which we constantly aspire

Spurred by self-indulgent
greed and need
We convince ourselves
as if by whim
"It's all about me"
not about Him

but innately planted
within each heart it's known
fulfillment comes
from unconditional love
alone

All These

In every subset of category
Exists the truth and the individual
Sometimes in harmony
More often at odds

Patronizingly invoking a mention of God
brings you neither closer to Him
nor nearer to the reality of truth.

His benevolence allows us to grapple with self
As if our issues concerned all else
beyond a relationship with Him.

Recognition, His quest
Service, His desire
Understanding, His goal
Compassion, His nature
Mercy, His gift
Redemption, His reward
All these given,
for belief.

Apple Core

'She made me do it'
he told the judge
'she was tempted
and then succumbed'

"So she gave right in
without a fight?
That's what you're saying,
Am I hearing you right?"

'That's correct, sir
she knew it a lie
and I think she knew
the whole damn time'

'She said
it wouldn't wash
Not with you sir,
but that didn't
for one minute
stop her'

'No sir,
she was convinced
she could have it all,
then proceeded to shackle me
chain and ball'

"So you tried to refuse
her advances
her wanton ways?"
"For how long was this,
an hour, a day?"

'Ah, to be exact
I don't recall
Remember I mentioned
that chain and ball?'
'I tried to get away
but she was so beguiling
I had to stay'

"So you told her outright
you told her 'No' ?"

'Well, she's a temptress
That's for sure
You know she's all woman
not a little girl'

"My question was
did you tell her 'No'
in no uncertain terms,
Explaining to her
you are both here
new lessons to be learned"

'Oh yes sir!
That was it,
but you know her
her voice is like a lair'

"So she dragged you down,
down to the ground?
You resisted, you kicked
you screamed?"

'Yes, that's it,
it was your previous instructions
to her I preened'

"So in summation,
you resisted
you tried
She convinced
she lied?"

'Correct sir
she overwhelmed me with words
It was in the way she acted,
She held it out
I retracted'

"However, you gave in
believing her to be right?
And then,
you,
took a bite?"

'Yes I admit it,
I thought I was free
to do that which I might'

"You listened to her
instead of me
Your actions
I wanted to forgive,
but then when on my walk
I called out,
you hid"

"Why didn't you come out
and admit to your transgression,
apologize and explain
that you had learned your lesson

Then ask forgiveness
of my redeeming love
Instead of refusing responsibility
and passing the buck"

"For the balance of your life
you shall toil without rest
and for your efforts
to place blame somewhere else
My sentence upon you,
is death"

Bull's Eye

How Lord
can we possibly
stand before you?

You know
of those things hidden,
veiled within our hearts
The jewels
and precious stones of sin
bedecking our crown
of lusts and cravings
To you suspicions? No
Your awareness is
right on the mark

An arrow already flown
it's perfect placement
suddenly shattered,
its shaft splintered
by one even more precise
following in its path

So exacting is your knowledge of us,
our sinful nature
wishes and desires

There is but one way
for us to have avoided
our unrepentant acts
Thereby being held accountable
for nothing
That would be, not to be;
To have never been born again

Then our loss
would be two fold
First, we would know nothing of you
Then, we would believe ourselves sinless
and in no need
of your redemptive love and compassion

Conquest

Today we celebrate
the greatest conquest of all
for the human race
The victory over death
and a guarantee of life everlasting.
For only the power of God's love
would be so immense
that He would make His only Son
our sacrificial lamb.

~An Easter Blessing

Conversant

Lord, it has been so long since we've talked,
I wonder why that is

The peace you reveal
quiets all other clamorous desires
and transcendent attempts
to fill my heart
Yet it is not until I am here again
with you
I realize and remember

Understanding you are always available
it is I who become caught up
in the ways and means of my world

I awake to stare at the eyes in the mirror
seeing me, not you
with plans of the day ahead
and their impending struggles
As ominous as the unseen beast
waiting to spring from the shadows
to wrestle life away from me
Devouring my self importance
Draining the spirit coursing through my veins

As if a wanderer
bedazzled by the vibrant colors of the jungle
Myopically through its façade
a false sense of security prevails
Straying from the veneered path,
not until lost
do my trembling thoughts refocus upon you
as my pleadings begin
And there you are
reminding me,
be still
be calm
for I AM here

Evening arrives and my exhaustion is palatable
Reflections of disparaging events and offenses
occupy both mind and body
as my spirit cries out silently

Extricating myself from worries
which exert feigned control,
hoping that in dream
my soul might be recharged
once more by yours
A renewed communion of spiritual energy
as we were before

Convicted

You make me believe that reward
is tied to obedience
You lead me to think blessings
are tied to understanding the Word
You convince me that elevated recognition
is grounded in good works
You charge me with fellowship
that I might come closer through others
I watch the rabble of the world
satiating themselves
yet I am convicted by pangs of guilt
even before I have faltered
You condemn me for the very thought of
straying
and still
you tell me He is an all forgiving and loving
God

He tells me His reward
is in my obedient belief
He informs me understanding the Word
is the blessing
He shows me the good work
recognized by His elevation upon the cross
His rejoinder to me *is* fellowship with His Spirit
I am tempted by unscrupulous gaiety
unaware of the gilded pain
lying in wait of their fall
He compassionately forgives,
saving me from condemning thoughts
each time I turn to Him

You claim to be men of God
He *is* the God of men

Crowns

how is it Lord
You, unseen, unheard
yet the fulfillment
within my heart
is as no other
when You are in my thoughts

the peace and understanding of our roles;
yours and mine
is at no time
more precise, more clear
than when You bless me
with a communion
of our two spirits

it is when You invite me
to rediscover your presence
within my life and world
that your crown of glory
takes its rightful place
in my heart
above all carnal and material desires

it is these meditative moments of reflection
one by one
like droplets of water upon limestone
which wear away and erode
the rough porous surface of my existence
revealing the smooth void created,
which once more may be filled
only with and by You
its creator

Days of Endearment

Nothing has changed
in the nature of man
except that he does,
when caught in the grip
of the devil's hand

We chase the dollar
three hundred, sixty five days a year
and set aside a few
for our Lord endeared

None is willing
to close the door
Simply said,
all three want more

Debt Free

What will we do
when the notes come due
on the house, the car
on our coveted
usury interest credit cards

How will we respond
to a sixty day pay and stay,
or Out!?

Where will we turn for help
As family, friends
every acquaintance we've known
even total strangers
seek our assistance and relief
from the strangle-hold grip
of their debt millstones

Who will we sacrifice
or be forced to give up
to extend for a while
the ever growing bills
on our 'past due' pile

How did it get this bad
this out of control
Consuming to impress
friends and neighbors,
ones we hardly know

Are we so ignorant
as to not understand
it all must come to an end
No material gain is ever enough
to set us totally free

Our choice one day
will be a simple one
Announce our intention to serve
God or Magog,
When that day arrives
both will mean death
but only one will bring eternal rest

We keep consuming
with reckless abandon
things we don't need
but won't live without
Trained to desire
and never tire
Accumulating more
from Babylon's whore

Sliding further into debt
To discover our future's
one sure bet
Satan stands ready
to take all I.O.U.'s
freeing us, clearing our slate
If we'll trade our cross
for the mark of the beast
to step through hell's
forsaken gate

Doubts

I don't know how to pray
I don't know what to say

"open thine heart" He says
"My words will speak to you
Put we two in our proper places
that's your job to do"

I don't know how to pray
I practice night and day

Connect often with the Spirit
for that's what we're told He is
Living within heart and soul
His desire for each
eternal life to win

I don't know how to pray
It never comes out the right way

There are always two ways
to go in life
with each decision's growth
Our focus, immediacy
and its relief
from our turmoil and its strife

I don't know how to pray
With my life I know I'll pay

There's His way
or there's our way
therein lies the pivotal position
The first step upon two parallel paths
holding the power of life or death

I don't know how to pray
I'm not sure what to say

Planted here by His loving hand
in body's fertile ground
seedling sown
maturity grown
self surrendered
His love
then known

I don't know how to pray
My words they stay at bay

Express your love
for all you see
is part of one glorious plan
His design, His purpose
His truth and love
for and within
each woman and man

I don't know how to pray
but from my heart, I start
today

End Times

Eight of ten horns
Now in place
Two more to go
Time to pick up the pace

Two formal states
now only debate
Their history filled
with suspicion and hate

'Roadmap to Peace'
Anti-Emmanuel soon released
Awaiting his invitations
amends to make
on his path of intentions

Armies assembled
both east and west
Caustic spark?
anyone's guess

Come to aid, to the rescue
To lead, to stand in the gap
Reconciler for the Jew
Leader of the trap

Patiently waiting
groomed for lies and deceit
In the wings
preparations for worldly feats
One like us
master of earthly tricks
His nemesis' sign
six six six.

Final Flight

What a trip
it's going to be
to leave the body
finally

A soaring spirit
once again
no longer occupant
of a flesh and blood pen

What once seemed
so permanent,
turning to dust
or ash
As essence,
spirit
flies free,
free at last

No longer afraid
frightened
or scared
No longer anxious
of the soul being bared

For each
and everyone
an accounting
will take place
For every living being
of what once was
a human race

All will have a chance
to stand before the assemblage of heaven
Explaining their actions
and responses
without ego, or self inflation,
as if bread
unleavened

And what will you say
on that last judgment day?
Claim ignorance
Misguided perseverance
Complicated resistance
What?. . .
Led astray?

Or willful disobedience
in the belief
you would never have to pay?

God has drawn
a line in time
and only He knows
its reason and rhyme

The Light
of His judgment day,
holds a dark of night
for all who will not
find His Way
before their final flight

Fire Dancer

The heat
the smoke
the flames that dance
Around my feet
they gently prance
The searing pain
of burning flesh
All,
put me to the test

Peeling back
layer upon layer
The explosive singe
of burning hair
Tied and bound
i do watch
As i become
a human torch

May i become
a radiant light
To show those caught
and trapped by the night
The justice reward
for sins not atoned,
My soul now looking
for its new home

A home above
Below
or beneath
Or cast among the gnashing teeth
The moans
the groans
the wailing
and tears,
forever is . . . how many years?

Alone,
forgotten
and now to be tossed
Upon the heap
with others as lost

Separated,
from Father
Son
and Holy Spirit
Your Gospel story,
just once more
could i hear it?

This time i would listen
understand
and obey
The love and desires
of the One who did say

"I love you forever
and for one more day
If only you would have
chosen my Way"

"My Son did I send
that you each might know
There is but one path to follow,
One way to go"

"To reach me once more
after all your trips
back and forth
that you might not miss"

"Your final escape
your final decision,
your final choice
without rescission"

"With just one thought
one word
one deed,
you could have shown
your true belief"

"Out of my love
I tried
and tried
And all you could do
was continue to lie"

"To lie, cheat and steal
is the world's common way
Its way of life,
each day until decay"

"To murder,
to covet
and to attack
Worse than all these
was to turn your back"

"On Me
on My Son
on My Spirit
My Love...
All
had been sent
for you from above"

i wouldn't listen, i wouldn't hear
the words which came to both my ears
Yes i heard but did not know
It was me in the balance
between above and below
It was, i thought . . . all about me
Not about He who hung on that tree
Taking my place once and for all
My ego now no longer stands tall

The me of this world now passing away
My soul all alone, wanting to stay
With you oh Lord, had i only obeyed

Food for Thought

How far away, are two
are we?

How much more time,
'til we are to meet?

How long,
will it be

before we two,
are both set free?

Fourteen generations,
Fourteen
and fourteen more?

When will you rest
on that velvet floor?

Are we two destined
to be together

or will our experience
co-exist never?

Awaiting your death
Awaiting my birth
Awaiting our introduction
In mother earth

How long before
we are both fed
You, God's fulfillment
You, my daily bread

For you are made man
Fated to die and decay
And I am made worm
Fated to hasten
your wasting away.

Forgotten

Their service illustrious
for what they went through
Their sacrifice immense
bathed in red white and blue

A background player promoting
God's crusading emissary
Forerunner of what tele-evangelism
might truly be

A generation plus gone by
old men now turned history
clutching, grasping desperately
to notoriety's identity

Still riding a wave that crested
and now merely laps on the sand
a faded memory for all
except to those who were part
of that brotherly band

Chained and shackled
by refusals to let go,
to grow
sliding on coat tails long ago forgotten
An imagined time they believed
would ever last
their once facile appearance now aged
by clinging to the past

And The World Moved On

Frustration

The most frustrating times
Jesus ever faced
had nothing to do
with the cross
or saving
a sinful human race

If His days were
anything like ours
His greatest task
daily was found
dealing with self-centered hypocrites
from sun up, to sun down

His tests of faith
were not in belief,
Was He or Was He Not?
regarding His role
as savior,
His faith was grilled
with regularity
by acts of self-indulgence
and its corresponding behavior

These He accepted as part of the job
Understanding man's selfishness
'goes with the territory'
you might say,
same as today

The one that required
His patience in this life
was confronting self-righteousness people
of every stripe

In virtually every instance
of contact He had
He was kind
and gentle
and seldom walked away mad
However, even He became frustrated
with mankind's propensity
for selfish impropriety

He never responded
with hate or revenge
or a pharisaic 'Jonesing' one-up-manship
Nor did He ever reply
in a tone of sass or lip
He'd simply suggest
"those who have ears,
let them hear"

"Love and truth
and compassion, please
It is with these
you will win your release"

Now realize,
understand
and marvel at,
in every instance
His response was consistent
Never giving up
giving in
or saying 'get a grip'

Never chiding with a yell
'go to hell'

Never asking
'now really, please'
Never exclaiming
'give me a break'

Forgiveness was exhaled
in every breath
He did take

Want to use Jesus
as your example today
of true Spiritual Christianity?
Then every single time
someone makes
a bone head mistake
or does something idiotic
or is selfish and rude
Stop,
and truly remember
what Jesus would do

Imperfect Balance

There is only one
who delights in our sin
more than we,
and that is the Devil himself

To him
the bitter aftertaste
of our guilt
is as sweet
as the anticipation
of our own unrepentant commitment

When we rebel
against the moral directives
of the Lord
the further our separation
from God becomes

Unable to establish
perfect balance between the two
We are ever moving
closer to one
and farther from the other

Inseparable

Each holiday and season
brought requests and gifts
Toys, candies, clothes and games
electronics, equipment
newer models, more of the same

Coveted material things
under trees, in bags
most wrapped, others not
expectant exchanges, symbols love fraught

Where are those prized possessions today?
What closet, attic, basement or trunk
keeps them safe, protecting their aging
promoting their wasting away

the "have to haves" of so long ago
the "I can't live withouts" for one more day
how much time, money, energy was invested
to be 'first on the block'
to be 'the one never bested'

And now?
What can I possibly give, promote or desire
that of itself you will never tire
Guaranteeing our continuance
as spiritual parent and offspring
what singular gift to you can I bring
One of encouragement, responsibility
to exhibit love's true encapsulating civility

None past nor present
nay, not one
can stand in comparison,
to the one I wish to share
for you to own,
to spend eternity with you
before the eyes on God's throne

It's All About He

There is a key
to success in this life
It's both sharp and hard
like the blade of a knife

When you are blessed
with something good
thank the Lord above,
for He remembered you
as He said He would

If tragedy or pain should strike
from afar or out of the blue
thank the Lord above again
for He was thinking of you
It's part of the way He allows
to mention
that He's trying
to get your attention

In either case
there is contained a lesson
about God's involvement in life
His goal is to help you
stay on the path
The one of love and compassion
Not the one which ends with His wrath

So remember tomorrow
whether good or ill
makes its visit on you
God is waiting
to see where you'll turn
and exactly what you'll do

Good or bad
will you trust and thank Him
to help see you through,
or once more rely upon yourself
believing,
it's all about you

Knowledge

The most valuable thing in the world
is knowledge,
from it, all else springs into being

Ideas are the seedlings
of knowledge
Intellectual properties
the living waters
of nurture and growth
Which, through expression
the world as we know it
comes into existence,
In an ongoing evolution
of progressive application
we use, abuse
and build upon

It is knowledge which creates
problems, their solutions
and new challenges

Knowledge;
The man without it
struggles
The man with it
toils
The man who mixes it
with spiritual understanding
and an acknowledgment of God
may be blessed to experience wisdom

Light

The waves crash
upon the rocks
spray, in the air
The tides continue to ebb and flow
always, without a care.

White caps on the horizon's peak
as if flickering off and on
One moment above the surface
the next moment gone.

To gaze out upon its spectrum
spectacle and might
The waters climb and roll
ever changing in their height
Its majesty combined
for my sight
Seeing the small me in perspective
is a thought of awesome fright.

To be lost at sea
no more than a speck
No power or control
to save my neck.

To the depths
do I commit
my mind, my body, my soul
What once was, is, to be no more
That which has always been
free again to soar.

To bob starkly alone
in the dead of night.
Drifting as smoke
lost in flight

Darkness,
despair
loneliness
fright
Waiting for a vision
A sign
A ship
to come
within sight.

Oh to be saved
one way or the other
To be warm and dry
in the arms of another
Reduces the fright,
darkness of night
For from up above
I am seeing a light.

Living Loving Memory

Leaving hearts behind broken
in these mourning moments of time
Grief weighs immeasurably down
upon these present
emotions and minds

Sensing your spirit
among us once more
Our loss overwhelming,
yet put away. .

By remembrance of your smile
ever brightly beaming

Your body at rest
Your soul gliding free
Peace now shrouding protectively
the new essence of your being

Your time here so fleetingly passed
still hard to imagine you're gone
In glory waiting patiently
for our journey's end . .
to join you before the throne

Love Lost

Loving behavior?
few and far between
Holding of hands?
lost esteem
Love light shining
betwixt four eyes?
Give in, Gave up
not worth the time

Love today?
a word bandied about
on movie screens,
in real time most likely
domestic screams

Couples sharing
dishonor, distrust
Histories of ex-es
past personal baggage
Single digit months
then evidence of corroding rust

Love today?
without depth
objects
adjectives
a synonym for sex
An empty emotion
trying to be filled
by 'Benjamin C-Note' power
and anti-depression pills

Love is meant to be
unconditional
Full of forgiveness
and compassion
To share, give and learn from
Not to be used
abused
held hostage,
penalized or rationed

Love is not of the mind
although we like to think it is
Love is not a physical urge
though its pain
can bring even the mighty down

Love is a soul connection
of spiritually charged energy
to be given freely
received fully
and shared faithfully

Love Potion

Thank you Lord for all you do in my life
My desire is that you would prod me
closer to you
for it is there, with you
fulfillment of my heart is accomplished

Knowing it is not your nature
nor your design to force
you allow us each to interact with you
of our own free will,
to be closer to you . . .
Or not

Name

I called your name

You heard
but would not listen
I wanted you christened

You, too busy chasing fame.

I spoke to you quietly

You heard
but would not heed
I offered to lead

You, turned away silently.

I came,
Again
and again
You wished only
to sin,
and sin.

You, turning
this way and that
Me, refusing to give up
leaving you flat

Remain a captive
and follow your lust
or come,
join the three of us

What will it take,
for you to see

All I want,
is to set you free.

So stand alone,
or become one with we three

For I have a plan
for each to hear
I have a path
for those who draw near
Open your mind
see what is clear
Know there is nothing
more to fear.

Your heart always knows the truth
Your heart never needs more proof

For you, for them,
it's all the same
I treat all alike

I simply, called your name.

New Now

For the Christian
who claims
now the Word to know
and new found righteousness
to the world
now to show
For the Born Again now
a new path to tread
For he and her
with new ecclesiastic pronouncements
now filling their heads

His challenge new, now proclaimed;

For the Christian
now to start
Revealed to the Christian's
understanding new heart
His followers now new
daily chore,
"Go, and sin no more"

Noetic Conversation
Mind Talk (*w/God*)

me
me
me
me
me
me,
You

(Yes)

my needs
my wants
my true desires

(I Know)

Like blue flames
of red raging fires

(You)

Love
Understanding
Compassion
Forgiveness; All free

(Learn)

Hidden behind veils of being one
other than me

(My Will)

To be at rest

(My Ways)

From my ways
From my work

(My Word)

From my words
From the daily struggles

(My Son)

With which I flirt

(All Given)

Please, please
Give me rest

(For You)

From all this pain
From all this hurt

Eternally.
(Eternally).

Omnivision

There are unseen eyes
watching each of us
from near yet oh so far

Tears are shed
droplets of sorrow
for pains suffered yesterday
today and tomorrow
Other glares
are of disgust
for actions of greed
and self-centered lust

With omnipresent sight
He sees all of these
and every single possibility
In each heart
In each mind
Into each reality

God's unseen eyes
see all there is
of every living thing
Nothing escapes His view
Not the ancient
Not the new

Omniscient
compassion, understanding, forgiveness. . .
why is it
so many people need these three
and instead for self, put them asunder

We may believe
we have hidden
in the darkness
of heart and mind,
our sinful mistakes
all judgment errors,
yet in truth
there is no valid excuse
for our disobedient acts

Without His omnipotent love
and guiding sight
Day would never
have evolved from night
Safety would be
obscured by fright
and mankind would not know
His Holy Light

We hope and pray He may not know
not one will He find out
but those unseen eyes
which see all there is
and ever now have been,
lovingly wait
for us to look
finally seeing Him

One Bottle of Beer, One Cup of Coffee

The world over
two men sit
sharing thoughts
of days past
Events they swore
would ne'er be forgotten
Times they believed
which would always last

Against a backdrop
of what once was reality
blended memories blur
Trying now to recall
adventures, escapades, stories
Moments of pain
Moments of glory

Those which have become
both faded
and exaggerated
Struggling for their rightful place
Fighting for their existence
like WW II's celebrated
insurgent resistance

Each mind's exercise
Each day's attempts to revive
Long awaited
and remembered dreams
Those which once were,
are still,
and hope yet to be seen

And all the while
each soul marches
stealthily onward
Its singular goal
to be washed clean

Each picture
Every line
All etchings,
Clean slate
Preparations for
a new birth arrival
at heaven's gate

Open

Open my mind Lord
that it might be filled with you
Open my heart
that it might be filled anew.
Open my eyes Lord
to see the truth
Open my arms
that they might receive a hint of you.
Open my shell Lord
to release my soul
Let my spirit fly through your universe whole.
Open my essence Lord and let it be
Allow me to serve
your name eternally.

Purpose

Everything in nature
serves a purpose

Man's blessing and bane
is to be the one creature
who can sense
the purpose served,
is to come closer to God
and to His Word

Life's credibility built
one statement at a time,
searching;
one thought remembered

Not knowing its import
or longevity,
while seldom realizing,
what it will be

All wanting approval,
need,
for and from others
family, friends, lovers

Recognition

In the battles of ego;
Identity

Epitome of righteousness;
humility

Kenosis brings enlightenment;
clarity

For when we are empty
we are once again pure

We stand before your throne
sensing our miniscule place
Condemned to understand
through the enormity of your love;
not chastising,
it is a love of forgiveness

We accept with honor and gladness
your command to do,
to be our best.

At once we are awake
forgetting our nocturnal eve's promise made
preparing for another day
of temporal tests

Relationship

Where God is
There is forgiveness
Where forgiveness is
There is understanding
Where understanding is
There is compassion
Where compassion is
There is a shared sense of vulnerability
Where this shared sense exists
There is knowledge of oneness
Where oneness dwells
There is a communion of love
Within a commune of love
Truth may thrive
Where truth is
The essence of spirits
Identify with each other

This is why I love you

Self Revelation

It's all about
the little me

Shelby Bright Eyes

My old dog and I
take a walk everyday
To the mailbox and back
the two of us stray

Come rain or shine
the two of us go
Sort of hand in paw,
don't you know

She hobbles down hill
I hobble up
Seems like just yesterday
we were both pups

Having a pet
is a glorious thing
As we look each other in the eye
I could swear both our hearts sing

That dog's a protector
whether I see her or not
No one comes near our property
without getting caught

Now she's too old to bite
and too old to fight
And she would never, ever attack
To tell the truth
most of the time
she's a little laid back

But I'll guarantee
all times day or night
If she senses alarm
or that something's not right
She'll sure as hell bark
and raise such a clatter
I'll know a stranger is here
and that's all that matters

I love that old dog
and I know she loves me
And together we make
a pretty good we

It's been said that a dog
is man's best friend
and that they'll be faithful
right up to the end
Having owned quite a few
I tend to agree
Dogs must have been put here
for you, and for me

All part of a plan
A plan of His
for we all know
what DOG
spelled backward is.

Skin Deep

Medical data retrieval
sounds innocent enough
Offer it for free
they'll all line up

A tiny Microchip
oh so thin, planted
just beneath the skin
Ply them with guilt responsibility each
every woman and man
Explain it will help find
those lost, abandoned

Market it
like a wanton tattoo
Having one will make you hip,
"you'll be so hot,
so cool"

Update the data
annually, free of charge
Offer frequent flyer miles,
or green stamp points
to be saved and used
to buy a new car

Make it a sin or a crime
a highly embarrassing shame
To be last on your block
walking around
without a registered microchip name

Then when it's time
to be scanned and checked
for the Mark of the Beast
all will be pre-assigned,
subcutaneously

Soul Resignation

World's design
stimulus,
ergo
response

Past regrets
Future's fear unknown
Today's besiegement
Seeds of control
in conflicts sewn

Mind's design
Physical desire
Soul's respite
flesh and bone soon to retire

All work completed
All races run
All tasks depleted,
accomplishments done?
accomplishments none.

He who dies
with or without
still does he die
Spirits fly
Bodies cry
Minds query
wondering why

Words resound
Lessons taught
Examples shown
Fellowship sought

The way He walked
The things He did
The legacy He left

What was His purpose?
According to who's plan?
Where leads the path
that recaptures the man

Surrender

the intentions you have for me
are greater than those I envision for myself

the plans you've made
fulfill more abundantly
than all I may have schemed

the dreams you've imagined for me
make mine pale in comparative reality

the goals you've set require
I look outside myself

the intentions
the plans
the dreams
the goals;
all opportune moments to come closer to you
now,
and eternally

Tapestry

At the end
we wonder
Where could we have done more?
and why didn't we?

With so much energy used
pursuing self
as if that truly mattered

The macro of I am
which dominated the landscape
from horizon to horizon
is marginalized to a micro of mass
on the verge of imploding
into the nothingness of a cosmic spark

Each leaves an imprint.
For whom and to what degree
it touches
or changes
the future,
is never known

Being no more than a mosaic speck
in the evolutionary tapestry,
designed and planned
to bring each life
once again
back to its creator

Testing

After all else failed
she relented, turning to God
Now she sees His handiwork
evidenced in every nuance

Each conversation belabors
His guiding, directive ways
like the thrashing grasp
of a drowning man
She longingly prays
enough impassioned verbiage
will convince herself of what
she misunderstands

A cure for all ills
The remedy for turmoil's strife
perhaps an answer for hereafter
but more importantly today
a stopgap to her slide

Yet hidden beneath
the brocade of her speech
a doubter's denial
rooted well within reach
That she might return
to her worldly wanton ways
should He fail her relief request
from the festering tests
of the choices she has made

Thank Yous

Thank you Lord
for allowing me to struggle
with your Word
with your Will
with your Ways
That I may no longer struggle
with those of my world
this new day

Mahalo for allowing me
to wait upon your ways
that I no longer carry
upon these small shoulders
the weight of the worlds
I once did crave

Danke Schoen for allowing me
to come before you
that I might kneel
in reverence to your will
That from this day forth
my heart may be
newly filled

Merci Beaucoup for allowing me
to know better your word
that those I so selfishly vent
might become mute
for their irrelevance

Gracias for allowing me
a heart and mind
filled with your presence,
to understand
I am not alone
in this time and place
and never have been

Arrigato for allowing me
to come back this time
As if I'd never left your side
for you, have never left mine

Thank you Lord
for remembering me
That I might never forget you

The Most Important Words

Ten. Love God first and most,
      treat your neighbor as yourself

Nine. If you knew me,
       you would know my Father

Eight. You can not serve both God and money

Seven. I am the resurrection and the life

Six. The truth will set you free

Five. Go and sin no more

Four.   This is my son

Three. Love each other

Two. Jesus Christ

One God

The Nature of Things

The leaves sing your praises Lord
as winds from your breath
rustle limbs and branches,
whispering to us
of life and of death

Your tears
rain down on us
the more we stray
the farther we drift
from your loving way

The stars above us
in the day's night sky
are as seeds you have sown
with a wave of your hand
That we might see them
from each and every land

Nature in this world
speaks only of you
Since the beginning
that has been true

Of course all that changed
once man made his things
in his own name

The ones you made
still honor and bow
The ones man made
demand kowtow

You sent us a servant
to show us the way
The way back to you
with each new day

A simple plan really,
when each night is done
with each new day's rising,
acknowledge the Son.

Three Year Tour

Here's a proposition
for your consideration,
say you could live
your dream
whatever it may be
You could be rich
or famous,
respected
or loved
You could excel
in any endeavor
field and occupation,
or none of the above

What if you were
independently wealthy
and could do nothing at all
except, shop or fish or play

What if you could do
anything you wanted
would an offer such as this
be of interest to you?

As you are aware
each coin has two sides
With that in mind
what would you be willing to do
to have your dream come true?

Except,
at the end of year three
It would also be
the end of you

Would you choose your dream's
fulfilled enjoyment
if at month thirty-six,
your body be spent?
your soul be sent?

That's the choice
Jesus of Nazareth made
for himself
for you and yours
His dream to serve
His life to give up,
after His three year tour

Thus Sayeth the Lord

In lieu of each drop of blood we've shed
with each drop of ink we've added
through the markings we freely desired
The Lord bequeaths
to you and me,
one day each
with the objects of our devoted
pictorial idolatry

For you with the rose
it will be rosy,
except for those thorns
penetrating your soul
For the ones with dragons
or wild animals assorted
it may not be cozy
with the carnivorous cavorting

For inked Christians
their sins atoned,
yet they too will be accountable
before the throne,
where God
will mete out
His justice great
in light of His Word
Leviticus,
Nineteen: twenty-eight

Trade Traits

God
man of God

God's vocation;
Creation,
man of God;
representation

God's disdain;
sin, in all its form,
man of God;
attempts to walk
a path forlorn

God's blessing;
Eternal life,
man of God;
words to relieve
the hearers strife

God's son;
the Truth
the Life
the Way
man of God;
proof all
do indeed stray

God's benevolent grace;
Forgiving love,
man of God;
part of the human race
encouraged guidance from above

God's trinity;
First and last,
man of God;
accepted role as cast

God's responsibility;
Compassion
Truth
Salvation,
man of God;
God's example of
vocation
disdain
blessing
son
grace,
trinity's reconciliation

Trash and Treasure

A lone palm frond
hangs limp
from the heat
of a noon day sun
Yielding slowly
each day marks a journey
from green to burnished gold

Twisted by the wind
valiantly trying
Doing its best
to keep from dying

More water?
Shade from another
closely planted neighbor?
A cool evening breeze?
What would it take
to be revitalized,
to be redeemed?

Turned to mulch
to dust
to ash,
to be composted
as green waste trash

To be re-mixed,
in a eco- waste bin
Part of new life
for other seed
bud or bulb

Re-mixed
and born again

Tripping

From here
to there
to eternity,
How far exactly
would that trip be

Have we trod these paths
more than once
Many say yes
Others an emphatic NO
For a few
it's déja` vu

To travel the light fantastic
requires character of depth

Untrue
and unworthy
are three cents a copy
while originals, priceless
their value a subjective guess

You're an original
look around
not another like you to be found
You say
you want
to be a star
Understand
that's what you are

For your place
in the heavens
in this universe wide
is now guaranteed
to be on one side,
or the other

Within God's grasp
within His reach,
or separated by
gnashing teeth
For this life may be
that drop in the bucket
when compared
to your next reality

So heed
the Word well
and understand,
the truth
the choice
of a heaven
or hell,

is yours
is in your hands

Two Sided Coin

God allows struggle
turmoil and strife
that we may find opportunities
to remember He's there,
and here
We take baby steps
then over-powering strides
upon the paths
of smiles and tears,
which stretch before us
in this physical experience
we label life

Why, we ask
Why not, He replies
Would you that I
would not test all your lies
Since the beginning
when Adam ran and hid
and then blamed Eve
for the thing he did
Mankind has always
wanted a free ride
and that's why all of you
still run and hide

You refuse to realize
what you do
think and say
I always see
It's impossible to keep
your behavior from me
That's why I made the devil
the frightening and evil side
After all,
isn't that the point?

You each must choose
who will you serve
and please
We both will reward you
for whom you follow
and believe
his, eternal separation
from my eternal peace

Unconditionally Yours

The incomparable greatness
of God's holy love
is evidenced by his willingness
to serve each
from above

We Three

I was alone
in this universe whole
my desire, your presence
before my throne
for I AM God
and my choice was never
to be on my own

to be one with me
and see my face
each must inhabit
my sin free space

not a singular fleck
not one little speck
of sin
in my holy presence may be
and it is this that keeps each
separated from me

that you and I may be near
I have sent to you myself
my spirit dwelling within a form
humanity could recognize,
a few with your hearts
but most with your eyes

for he is, as I AM
the same spirit are we
purity did temporarily reside
in your den of sin
that each of you fully stained
might yet live again

my unconditional love was for him
as his is now for you,
through this love
both you and he
may now stand together
before me

for he was sinless pure
and put it aside
to redeem you and yours,
he took your penalty
paid the price
suffering death in your place

the manner by which
you come to me
is through my spirit given free,
to acquire said
to accept and join us
is in my son to believe;
that he is of me
that we are one
serving you
in the form of three

I've made it simple
for all to see
how easy it is
to be one with me
eternally

Writing professionally since 2001, story teller Branch Isole is the author of fifteen books. His style and presentation, known as 'voyeurism poetry' engages the reader in life themes often experienced but not always voiced.

Born in Osaka, Japan the son of a career military officer, Branch traveled extensively growing up, calling many places 'home'. Finishing high school in Southern California, Branch went on to graduate from Texas State University, attended graduate school at the University of Houston and received an M.A. degree from Trinity Theological Seminary.

Living on the island of Maui, Branch credits the juxtaposition of a modern world against the backdrop of the sophisticated raw nature and beauty of the Hawaiian culture, people and islands as his inspiration.

Branch Isole is the Voyeuristic Poet, sharing Mana'o* with individuals and groups.
His catalogue of work includes poetry, short stories and articles for journals, magazines, newsletters and on the Internet at www.manaopublishing.com.

*Mana'o (pronounced Ma Na O) is Hawaiian for 'Thoughts, Ideas and Opinions'.

Saccharin and Plastic Band Aids ©
Comments in Poetic Prose
ISBN 0-9747692-8-2